Anonymous

An Opinion of Counsel on the Action of the General Synod of the Reformed Presbyterian Church

Anonymous

An Opinion of Counsel on the Action of the General Synod of the Reformed Presbyterian Church

ISBN/EAN: 9783337296667

Printed in Europe, USA, Canada, Australia, Japan

Cover: Foto ©Lupo / pixelio.de

More available books at **www.hansebooks.com**

AN OPINION OF COUNSEL

ON THE

ACTION OF THE GENERAL SYNOD

OF THE

Reformed Presbyterian Church,

IN THE CASE OF

MR. GEORGE H. STUART,

AND

DOCUMENTS RELATING TO THE FIRST REFORMED PRESBYTERIAN
CONGREGATION IN THE CITY OF PHILADELPHIA.

Philadelphia, Sept., 1868.

Philadelphia:

JAS. B. RODGERS, PRINTER, 52 AND 54 NORTH SIXTH STREET.

1868.

OPINION OF COUNSEL.

WE have carefully considered the action taken by the Synod of
the Reformed Presbyterian Church, at its late Session in Pittsburg,
in the case of Mr. Stuart, and we shall proceed to state the con-
clusions at which we have arrived.

The suspension of Mr. Stuart from church membership and from
his office of ruling elder, and the vacation of his seat in Synod,
were sought to be effected by the passage of resolutions reciting the
offence and the law supposed to be violated and declaring the penalty
to be inflicted. Four series of resolutions were introduced for
this purpose, the last of which only was passed.

The Synod, as a legislative body, was competent to vacate Mr.
Stuart's seat for sufficient cause, but not for any cause whatever
to deprive him of church membership and of his office of ruling
elder. Only as a court could they effect that, and to do so it was
necessary that they should try, convict, and sentence him in accor-
dance with the laws they were constituted to administer.

We shall consider the case under the following heads :

1. The Charge.
2. The Jurisdiction.
3. The Process.

I. THE CHARGE.

The resolutions, which were passed, charge Mr. Stuart with the
commission of two acts, which they declare to be offences against
the well known and established laws of the church. They are,
first, the use in the worship of God " of imitations and uninspired
compositions, called hymns ;" *secondly*, communion "with others in
other churches in sealing ordinances."

A paper was also presented to the Synod, properly styled a
Libel, purporting to be signed by one Ephraim Young, and charg-

ing Mr. Stuart with lying, and with using "uninspired hymns contrary to the standards of the church."

The libel cannot serve as the foundation of the resolutions, for the charges contained therein are not identical with those set forth in the resolutions. The resolutions make no mention of the infamous charge of lying, and substitute therefor that of communing with members of other churches, nor does their statement of the charge of using uninspired hymns agree with that of the libel. The libel specifies the offence as that of using such compositions in a public meeting held in a Baptist Church, while the resolutions are so vague in their terms as to leave it uncertain whether the offence was committed in the religious services, public or private, of the Reformed Presbyterian Church, or by participation in the exercises of other bodies. Nor is their statement of the other charge, that of communion in other churches, more definite; for here they leave it uncertain whether the offence consisted in adoring the Host and receiving a consecrated wafer from the hands of a Roman Catholic Priest, or in partaking of the Lord's Supper in an Old School Presbyterian Church. The vagueness of the resolutions is the more to be regretted, for as no libel was framed by the Synod, no evidence adduced, no defence permitted, and no formal sentence pronounced, the resolutions constitute the whole record, and to them alone, therefore, can we look for a statement of the offence of which a majority of the Synod have pronounced Mr. Stuart guilty.

We do not propose to consider the question whether the rules of faith and practice of the Reformed Presbyterian Church forbid absolutely, and on all occasions, the singing, or inciting others to sing, uninspired hymns, and the participation with members of other Protestant Churches in the celebration of the Lord's Supper. It is sufficient to say, that, on both points, the teaching of the "Declaration and Testimony" of the church and the utterances of its judicatories are not clear and unambiguous, and that the practice of its members, both clerical and lay, has not been of sufficient uniformity to give a settled construction to those doubtful enactments.

There was an objection to the reception and consideration of the charges against Mr. Stuart which the Synod overlooked. Chapter

III., Sec. 1, § 7, of the Book of Discipline of the Reformed Presbyterian, Church provides that "no charge shall be admitted against "any member of the church unless it be presented within *one* "year, in case of private members or ruling elders * * * after the "facts upon which the charge is founded have come to the know- "ledge of the accuser." The resolutions were general in their terms—they specified no particular act, and were founded, therefore, not on any particular offence, but upon an alleged habit. In all probability, no member who voted for them could say that the facts upon which they were founded had come to his knowledge within one year. The Book of Discipline, therefore, by the spirit, if not the letter, of this rule, prohibited the Synod from entertaining the charges.

II. THE JURISDICTION.

The first preamble to the resolutions affirms the original jurisdiction of the Synod over this subject. That it did not proceed by virtue of its appellate jurisdiction is certain; for the libel, signed by Ephraim Young, was not the basis of the synodical action, the charges therein not agreeing with those in the resolutions; nor had it been properly presented to the session of the First Church, and brought up on appeal. The Synod must, therefore, have taken cognizance of Mr. Stuart's alleged offences by virtue of their original jurisdiction, which is, however, not unlimited. The Book of Discipline, (Chap. III., Sec. 2, § 1,) restricts that jurisdiction to "cases "in which the inferior judicatories are remiss in the exercise of dis- "cipline, or otherwise incapable of applying a remedy to an open scandal." But, in order to vest jurisdiction in the Synod, some evidence should appear on the record of that remissness or incapability which has disqualified the lower courts, and entitled the Synod to act originally; or, at least, there ought to be an explicit finding by the Synod, as a condition precedent to its exercise of jurisdiction, that those facts existed; for otherwise the limitation on the Synod's jurisdiction would be wholly ineffectual, and they might exercise it at their will. In this case there is neither allegation nor evidence of such remissness or incapability on the part of the lower courts. There is simply, in the first preamble to the resolutions, a very general claim to "original as well as appellate jurisdiction over all

"persons and all matters affecting the general interests of the
"church under its supervision and care."

We are therefore of opinion that the Synod had not jurisdiction,
either original or appellate, of Mr. Stuart's case.

III. THE PROCESS.

Even if the Synod could properly have taken jurisdiction of the
case, the defects of their process were fatal to the validity of the
proceedings. Contrasting their proceedings, in this case, with the
rules for trials as laid down in the 2d section of the 3d chapter
of the Book of Discipline, it seems to be doubtful whether those
who voted with the majority in Synod had read that chapter.

It directs:

That the judicatory shall present a libel to the party accused, spe-
cifying the time and place of the offence and "allowing the accused"
if he himself desire it, at least one week to prepare for "trial." § 5.

That the judicatory shall not proceed, in the absence of the
accused, until he shall have been cited three several times, at such
intervals of time, as shall be reasonable to grant him, and shall
have been served with a copy of the libel. § 7.

That upon the appearance of the accused, the charge shall be
read to him, and, if necessary, explained by the Moderator. § 8.

That the accused, if he put himself upon his defence, shall be allowed to use all lawful means to clear himself of the imputation. § 9.

That witnesses shall be summoned, be examined, if either party
so require; under oath, and, in all possible cases, in the presence
of the accused. § § 10 and 11.

It is directed in the IV. chap. that, if found guilty and
ordered to be suspended, sentence of suspension shall be publicly
pronounced by the Moderator. Sec. I. § 3.

In this case no libel was framed nor presented to Mr. Stuart.
Three sets of resolutions were introduced They were vague and in-
definite in their charges, and specified neither the nature, time, nor
place, of the offence. Nor was a copy of any one of these resolutions
furnished to the accused. One hour's notice was given him of the
taking of the final vote, at a time, when, it is supposed, every member of Synod knew that he was ill and unable to be present.

Mr. Stuart put himself upon his defence and filed a formal denial of the charges in manner and form as alleged. No witnesses were examined either for the prosecution or the defence. No sentence of suspension was publicly pronounced by the Moderator.

Considered as a whole, this record, in our opinion, exhibits so great a departure from the requirements of the Book of Discipline, and from the established principles of jurisprudence, as to render the proceedings entirely invalid.

CHRIS. STUART PATTERSON,
WILLIAM A. PORTER.

Philadelphia, July, 1868.

DOCUMENTS.

THE General Synod of the Reformed Presbyterian Church commenced its sessions in Pittsburg, May 20th, 1868. On the following day, May 21st, an organization was effected, which was regarded as unconstitutional, and the following protest entered against it:

[A.]

PROTEST.

The subscribers respectfully protest against the organization of the General Synod of the Reformed Presbyterian Church at its sessions in Pittsburg, commencing May 20th, 1868, for the following reasons:

1st. Because, in the organization of said Synod, the delegation of a Presbytery, to wit: the Second Reformed Presbytery of Philadelphia, was admitted, its delegates were entered on the roll, allowed to vote, and one of them was elected moderator, although the Synod had no official knowledge whatever of the organization or existence of said Presbytery.

2d. Because it was alleged, and certified evidence of the fact was ready, and would have been given if allowed, that the said Second Presbytery, applying for admission, was not the Presbytery which Synod authorized and directed to be constituted, inasmuch as said Presbytery had, without authority, taken under its jurisdiction the Third Reformed Presbyterian Church, Philadelphia, a congregation, under the jurisdiction of the Reformed Presbytery of Philadelphia, which had never been dismissed by that Presbytery, and which said Second Presbytery had received under its jurisdiction, without any authority whatever from Synod, and without the knowledge and consent of the Presbytery, to which it properly and lawfully belonged.

3d. Because, when an appeal was taken from the decision of the moderator, that it was in order to accept and enroll the delegates

of the said Second Presbytery of Philadelphia, the moderator refused to put the appeal, although rule 25 of the rules for General
Synod and other judicatories, expressly states that, "if any member
feels aggrieved by any decision of the moderator, he may appeal to
the judicatory, stating reasons:" such appeal being allowed by all
parliamentary and ecclesiastical usage, and at the last meeting of
this Synod, in New York, 1867, an appeal being twice admitted
and put, in circumstances precisely similar, *to wit*, while the
question of organization was pending.

4th. Because an organization, by the choice of officers, could not
properly be effected until the members were ascertained, and until
the right of any, whose claim was contested, was decided, for which
purpose the moderator and clerk of the preceding Synod remain in
office and exercise their functions, so that the court may be able to
act in an orderly manner on such a subject.

5th. Because the certificate of a Presbytery is to be considered
as *prima facie* evidence of a right to sit as a member only when
such certificate is not disputed for reasons assigned: since cases might
occur, and have occurred, where an improper number of delegates,
or persons not regarded as having standing in the church, are
commissioned, as when Rev. Wm. Wilson, minister, and Thomas
Wilson and W. Taylor, elders, were not allowed to sit in Synod as
delegates from the Pittsburg Presbytery, (see minutes, 1850,) their
claim to sit, although duly certified, having been challenged by
Rev. A. W. Black: and it is evident that the allowing all who are
certified to sit, might take the control of the Synod out of the
hands of these to whom it truly belongs, and give it to an illegal
and unconstitutional majority when really a minority.

6th. Because the said Second Reformed Presbytery having unconstitutionally received the Third Reformed Presbyterian Church,
Philadelphia, while the said congregation was legally under the
jurisdiction of another Presbytery, and having thereby vitiated its
own organization, and thus ceased to be the Presbytery authorized
by Synod, the admission of the delegates of said Presbytery to
Synod violates the constitution and order of the church, and vitiates
the organization of this Synod.

7th. Because by the admission of said delegates of said Second
Presbytery of Philadelphia, a practical sanction is given to acts of

gross disorder, utterly subversive of the essential principles of Presbyterian polity; for, if the act of said Second Presbytery of Philadelphia, in receiving said Third Reformed Presbyterian Church, Philadelphia, under its care be allowed, said Second Presbytery of Philadelphia might receive, under its care, any congregation of any other Presbytery without the knowledge or consent of said other Presbytery, and without the authority of Synod, and thus said Second Presbytery of Philadelphia might extend itself to all parts of the Church, and appropriate congregations from any other Presbytery interfering in their just jurisdiction, and inciting and fomenting disorder and division throughout all the church.

8th. Because, by this action of Synod, the just rights of the Philadelphia Reformed Presbytery were practically violated, and the act of a congregation, which was grossly disorderly, was practically approved and ratified, and that without any investigation whatever.

9th. Because the constitution of Synod, which requires that the delegates from each Presbytery shall be persons under the lawful jurisdiction of the Presbytery, which sends them, was violated by the admission of a person as a delegate from the Second Reformed Presbytery of Philadelphia, who was an elder of a congregation not lawfully under the jurisdiction of said Presbytery.

SAML. WYLIE,
T. W. J. WYLIE,
GEO. H. STUART,
BENJ. MILLER,
JOHN MCMILLAN,
A. G. MCAULEY,
R. H. MACMUNN,
W. STERRETT,
ROBT. MCMILLAN,
GEO. SCOTT,
JOHN F. HILL.

On the afternoon of the same day, when the Minutes were read, it appeared that the objections made against the organization of the Synod had not been fairly and fully stated, and when the court refused to allow the statement of the person who presented the objections to be entered on the record in his own language, the following Protest was presented:

[B.]
PROTEST AGAINST MINUTES.

The subscribers respectfully protest against the action of General Synod in adopting the following record of its proceedings, to wit:

" When the certificate of delegation from the Second Reformed Presbytery of Philadelphia, the last presented, was read, Rev. Dr. Wylie objected to it, as the Presbytery was unconstitutionally organized."—

Because it was explicitly and repeatedly denied that it was stated that the Second Reformed Presbytery of Philadelphia had been unconstitutionally organized, but it was affirmed:

1. That the Synod had no official and sufficient knowledge that said Presbytery had been organized, and

2, (the foregoing objection being overruled), that the said Presbytery was *at the present time* unconstitutional, because it had vitiated its organization by the admission of a congregation properly belonging to another Presbytery, without the knowledge and consent of the Presbytery, to whose jurisdiction it properly belonged, and of this Synod.

A. G. McAuley,	Samuel Wylie,
R. H. MacMunn,	Benj. Miller,
W. Sterrett,	T. W. J. Wylie,
Geo. H. Stuart,	John McMillan,
John F. Hill,	Geo. Scott,

Robt. McMillan.

———

On the afternoon of Friday, May 22, as Synod was about to adjourn, the stated clerk announced that several papers were on the table, which he proceeded to read, without stating by whom or how they were presented, and notwithstanding objection was made to their reception as entirely out of order. These papers are as follows:

[No. 1.]

REMONSTRANCE.

We, the undersigned, Elders, Trustees and members of the First
Reformed Presbyterian Church, Philadelphia, appear in General
Synod as remonstrants, and ask for such relief from existing
grievances as your venerable Court can give, for the following reasons, viz.:

1st. At a congregational meeting, duly held on the 6th of January, 1868, the following persons were elected a Board of Trustees
for the current year:—George Gordon, Ephraim Young, Robert
C. Taylor, John Biggerstaff, James Stewart, James Graham, and
Thomas Johnston. On the following Monday the new Board met
and organized. The last two declined to serve with the new
Board, and they, in connection with two other members of the old
Board, changed the locks upon the doors and gates of the church
property, and, claiming still to be recognized as the Board *de facto*,
took possession of the property in this summary way, thereby
usurping the functions of a Board, and interfering with the election
held according to the charter and disturbing the peace of the congregation.

2d. At another congregational meeting, held February 13th,
1868, for the purpose, as was alleged, of hearing a report from the
session and members of the old Board, respecting the list of
electors, it was found that these self-constituted revisors of the list
had declared 127 persons to have voted illegally. When the
names of these persons were called for, they were refused, and

the chairman of the meeting, after putting the motion for the acceptance of the report, declared it to be carried, although a large majority was opposed to it, and refused to be a party to cutting off 127 persons, whose names were not given, and who, for aught that appeared to the contrary, had as good a right to vote as those who declared their votes illegal.

3d. Seeing no way open by which to recover their rights, as the majority of the session and its moderator seemed to have agreed to do what they could to deprive them of the same, the new Board resorted to a civil tribunal for redress, while, in the meantime, an injunction was obtained restraining the new Board from the exercise of its functions about the property, through the exaggerated and sworn statements of the pastor and others in regard to what might transpire in the event of the new Board collecting pew rents.

4th. After the suit in equity had been commenced, in order that all occasion for reflection might be removed, and a way opened up for prevention of further litigation, the new Board proposed to leave the whole matter to arbitration, the conditions being that both parties should choose each three disinterested ruling elders from the Reformed and United Presbyterian Churches, and that these were to choose a seventh; and that both parties should sign a paper to abide by the decision of the arbitrators. This proposition, with others previously made, was scornfully rejected, and it thus became painfully evident that those holding illegal control of the property did not desire either justice or a peaceable settlement.

5th. Notwithstanding earnest remonstrances and protests, the majority of the session, encouraged by the moderator, have, since the difficulties commenced, been pursuing a course calculated to destroy the comfort of the majority of the congregation, fan the flame of discord, and, unless arrested, tending to drive from the congregation the oldest and staunchest friends of the Church.

6th. The majority of the Session, instead of acting towards the congregation as a Court of Christ, and endeavoring to calm the troubled waters, have commenced a series of libelous proceedings against members of the same session, and members of the congregation, who differ with them on matters of principle. These proceedings have been conducted, for the most part, in secret session against the earnest wishes of the accused. In these secret conclaves *two*, among the oldest members of Session, have been tyrannically subjected to the unrighteous sentence of suspension from the exercise of office and the enjoyment of the privilege of membership, without libel, citation or trial. These unjust and unscrupulous acts, recounted, were greatly aggravated and intensified by the pastor's availing himself of his official position on the Sabbath, and from the pulpit to give a detailed one-sided statement of secular matters connected with the civil suit, accompanied with an unfair and disingenuous reference to four respectable members of the Church, one of whom was specially singled out, and an attempt made to cover his name with infamy in the presence of the assembled congregation. Thus the thrones of Israel, instead of being thrones of public interest and impartial justice, have been converted into star chambers, where character is murdered in the dark, and the friends of truth, order and principle are persecuted and held up to ridicule for their fidelity to their covenanted engagements.

7th. It is believed by your remonstrants that the difficulties with which we are now beset might be arrested by the faithful exercise of discipline upon some of those in the congregation, who, having lost their sympathy with the Reformed Presbyterian Church, are, by a repetition of disorderly acts, aiming to accomplish their destruction. It is currently reported that the pastor of the congregation joined in the dispensation of the Lord's Supper in the New School Presbyterian congregation, under the care of Rev. W. T. Wylie, Newcastle, Pa. Also, that he coöperated with an Old School Presbytery in the city of New York, in an act of ordination under peculiarly aggravated circumstances. And it is a well authenticated fact that he has repeatedly announced as matter of praise uninspired compositions, popularly styled hymns, thus as we conceive violating the standards of the Church, his ordination and other vows, and following divisive courses.

As it will appear from the above rehearsal that we can expect no redress from the session of the congregation—and when some of us applied for redress by appeal to our Presbytery, we were refused a hearing, the moderator from the chair declaring that we *had no right* to protest or appeal, not being *members of court*, and recognizing your original, as well as appellate, jurisdiction of the Church—we ask you in the name of the Head of the Church to interpose your authority, and give us such relief as you may deem proper.

8th. There can be no doubt, from all that has taken place in this Church during the last few years, that the foundation of our difficulties lies in a difference of sentiment in regard to Psalmody and Communion. Believing, therefore, that it is in the power of your venerable body to give effect to your decisions on these matters, we earnestly and humbly ask you, not only to abide by the standards as *they* are, but to call to an account those who are troubling this congregation by their tyranny in ruling, their defection in principle and their disorderly practices.

[The following list of signatures to the Remonstrance is taken from the Minutes of the recent Synod, with corrections of supposed typographical errors, and the omission of names withdrawn by request, as being obtained by incorrect representations of the nature of the document, and in a number of instances attached to it without the knowledge of the persons themselves. It appears that of those whose names were appended 4 were under suspension, 4 under process, 13 dismissed, 6 duplicated, 44 withdrawn, and 2 unknown,—a total of 73 improperly added :]

ELDERS.—Robert Guy [suspended], A. S. McMurray [suspended].

TRUSTEES.—George Gordon [under process], Ephraim Young [under process], James Stewart, Robert C. Taylor [under process], John Biggerstaff.

MEMBERS. — Samuel McGonegal, Mary McGonegal, Annie McGonegal, Eliza Noble, Samuel McMullen, Hannah McMullen, Letitia Gordon, Matilda Cochran, James Montgomery, Rachel Montgomery, Mary J. Taylor, Samuel Berk [? Beck], Martha A. Berk [? Beck], Sarah C. Boyd, David W. McElroy, Jane McElroy, Mary A. Gordon [? Jordan], John McLure, Jane McLure, Margaret Dysart, Mary Rodgers [duplicate], Robert Jordan, Eliza Jordan, Charles Williams, Robert Johnston, Robert Alexander, Matthew Cook, Mary Cook, Jane Johnson, Matilda Garrett, Thomas Pollock [dismissed], Jane Pollock, Catharine Donaghy, Robert Fletcher, Ann J. Fletcher, Mary Fletcher, Rose A. Conner, William Graham, Mary Graham, Robert Lithgow, David Donaghy, Lizzie Donaghy, Margaret Alexander, Mary A. Alexander, Maggie Alexander, Hugh Tait, Catharine Tait, William J. Jackson, Robert Robinson, Sarah Cannon, Jane Cannon, Eliza Cannon, Alex. Gamble, Isabella Gamble, Bella Gamble, Bella Moore, James Smyth, Jane Smyth, James Richie, Jane Richie, George Richie [dismissed], Mary Richie [dismissed], Mrs. Mary Richie, James McLeod, Ann McLeod, Margery Williams, Jane Williams, Margaret Williams, Anna Williams, William Archibald, Elizabeth Archibald, Samuel White, Elizabeth White, William McIlvain, Elizabeth McIlvain, Isabella Vallier, John Tait, Frances Tait, Robert Jackson, Jane Jackson, John Stewart [under charges], Hannah Adamson [dismissed], Ellen Andrews [dismissed], Jane Patterson [? John], A. Jane Stewart, Martha Stewart, Jane Hamilton, Mrs. Ellen T. McMurray, Sarah J. McMurray, Mrs. Eliza Jane Mitchell, A. Matilda Mitchell, Mrs. M. M. Pollock [? Kollock], Nancy Pollock, William Mooney, Jane Mooney, Margaret Mooney, Jane Smith, Maggie D. McDowell, Mary A. Smith, Mrs. Mary Matson, Mary O. Matson, Margaret J. Arbuckle, Elizabeth Potter, Mary Ann Miller, Jane Neely, Jane Potter, Martha Biggerstaff, John A. R. McLeod, Alex. Stewart, Mary Stewart, John Kane, Matthew Haggerty, Ellen T. Haggerty, Martha Crane [? Crozier], Mrs. Rosa C. Richie, Margaret Morrison, Martha A. Stewart, Sophia A. Loughead, Rachel Alcorn [dismissed], Mattie Alcorn [dismissed], Mrs. Isabella Sirte [? Sixte], Mrs. Isabella Cook [dismissed], Elizabeth Tamon [? Lamon], Charlotte Allen, Margaret Nolen, Barbara Richards, Mary A. Gibson, Margaret Huston [dismissed], Letitia Simpson, John Hagerty, Mary A. Love, Jane Morison, George Thompson, Anna E. Thompson, Robert Black, Margaret A. Black, James Kerr, Ann E. Kerr, Elizabeth Stewart, Elizabeth Phair, Barbara Graham, Rebecca Young, Andrew Christie [dismissed], Annie Christie, Isabella J. Christie, Isabella Taylor, Maggie H. Scott, Daniel Boyd, James Boyd, David Donaghue [? Donaghy, duplicate], Eliza Donaghue [? Donaghy, duplicate], Margaret Egan, George Thompson [duplicate], Eliza A. Thompson [duplicate], William Campbell, Andrew Lockhart, Ann Lockhart, Sarah Lockhart, Eliza J. Lockhart, John Johnson, Letitia Johnson, Martha Cromie, Thomas Cromie, Elizabeth Miller, Robert White, Martha

White, William Jackson, Sr., Margaret Gray, H. McConnell, A. McConnell, Thos. McCandless, Jane Orr, Margaret Graham, Mary Haggerty, Ann Haggerty, Henry Humphries [suspended], Mary Humphries [suspended], Robert Humphries, Mary Ann Humphries, John A. Anderson, Maggie Anderson, Mrs. Wm. Brewster, Annie Crow, Mary A. Crow, Mr. S. Gray [? Mrs.], Miss S. Gray, Charles Gray, David Foster [unknown], Mary A. Crawford, William Neely, Mary Ann Neely, Margaret Mackey, Dorcas Mackey, Ellen Watson, William VanCent [? VanZant], Jane VanCent [? VanZant], Andrew Moore, Jane E. Burrell [? Russell], Elizabeth Kerr, Jane Forsythe, Eliza J. Wiyine [? Wayne], James Fullerton, John Gibson, Elizabeth Gibson, James Taylor [dismissed], Letitia Taylor, Elizabeth Taylor, Mary Rodgers, Jane Mier [? Wier], Ann McTrusly [? McTrusty], Mrs. Emma McLaughlin, Daniel Love, Mary J. Love, Eliza McKay, Sr., A. J. McKay, Margaret McKay, Hugh McKay, Eliza McKay, Mrs. McKelvey [unknown], William Lithgood [? Lithgow], Jane Lithgood [? Lithgow], Samuel Boyd [dismissed], Jane Boyd [dismissed], Robert A. Johnson, Eliza Johnson, Catharine Lindsay, Ellen Kerr, James Orr, Hannah Orr, Ann Jane Orr, Joseph Drake, Martha G. Drake.

[Paper No. II. being a Memorial against the proposed union of the Presbyterian Churches, was laid on the table, and is not included in these documents.]

[No. III.]

LIBEL.

Whereas lying and corrupting the worship of God, thus following divisive courses, are sins against God, and a scandal to His church; and whereas you, George H. Stuart, are charged with said sins and scandals, by Ephraim Young, therefore you should be proceeded against by the censures of the house of God, designed as these are for your edification, and not for your destruction. The specifications of the charges against you are, that on the 13th of January, 1868, or thereabouts, in the First Ref. Pres. Church, Philada., you were guilty of lying in the following particulars, viz.: While the lately elected Board of Trustees of said church were leaving the lecture-room after having organized according to the

2

provisions of the charter, you shook your fist in the face of Robert C. Taylor, and demanded from him the keys, with the threat that if he did not give them up you, Geo. H. Stuart, had a writ filled in your hand, an officer at the door, and would in three minutes have him locked up; and, further, when Wm. Ray, President of the late Board, immediately afterwards made formal demand for the keys, you, Geo. H. Stuart, did state that you would give Robt. C. Taylor another opportunity to give up the keys, and again did threaten to have him locked up in Moyamensing that night if you had money enough to do it; or words to this effect. And, further, at a meeting of Session of said church, held in the pastor's study, Jan. 23d, 1868, or thereabouts, you, George H. Stuart, did positively deny, in presence of the Session, that you had used the language above specified in this libel.

Witnesses: George Gordon, John Biggerstaff, Robert C. Taylor, James Stuart, John M. Kolloch, M. D.

And, further, you, Geo. H. Stuart, did on March 10th, 1868, in the Baptist Church, corner of Broad and Arch Sts., Philada., give out as chairman of the meeting, uninspired hymns, contrary to the standards of this church, thus corrupting divine worship, and acting in a manner calculated to produce alienation and dissension among brethren. Witnesses: John Martin, John Chambers, Mrs. Mary M'Bride, Miss Lizzie M'Bride, John Tait. With all this you are charged, and an opportunity is now offered of presenting your defense, if any such you have to make.

EPHRAIM YOUNG.

Philada., April 23d, 1868.

That this is a correct copy of a document presented to the General Synod of the Reformed Presbyterian Church, is certified by

JOHN N. McLEOD,
Stated Clerk.

[No. IV.]

LIBEL.

Whereas corrupting divine worship, following divisive courses, and *lying*, are sins against God and a scandal to his church, and whereas you W. J. Chambers are charged with said sins and scandals, by Geo. Gordon, therefore you should be proceeded against by the censures of the house of God, designed as these are for your edification, and not for your destruction. The specifications of the charges against you, are that while conducting the worship of God in the Wylie Mission Sabbath School of the 1st Ref. Pres. Church, in South street below Thirteenth, Phila., of which you were lately superintendent, you used uninspired hymns, contrary to the 8th section of the 24th chap. of our Testimony.

Witnesses, Abraham Walker, Charles Williams, Jr., Miss Margaret Williams, Miss Lizzie Kerr and Francis McBride.

And further, that in January 1867, or thereabout you boasted to a brother, that you would revolutionize this church, thus declaring your purpose to violate your ordination vow. Witnesses, Wm. B. Hill, John Tait, David Hazel, Robt. Jordan and Robt. Alexander.

And further, that when you were charged with this in a congregational meeting, held in the 1st Ref. Pres. Church, Phila., on the 20th of Nov., 1867, or thereabouts, you publicly denied that you had so boasted.

Witnesses, William McIlwain, Robt. Jordan, John Tait, David Hazel, James Smith, Robert Alexander.

With all this you are charged, and an opportunity is now offered of presenting your defense, if any such you have to make.

GEORGE GORDON.

Philadelphia, April 23, 1868.

That this is a correct copy of a document presented to the General Synod of the Reformed Presbyterian Church is certified by

JOHN N. McLEOD, *Clerk.*

[No. V.]
LIBEL.

WHEREAS, Corrupting divine worship, and thus following divisive courses, is a sin against God, and a scandal to his Church; and

WHEREAS, You, James Grant, are charged with said sin and scandal, by Ephraim Young; therefore, you should be proceeded against by the censures of the house of God, designed as these are for your edification, and not for your destruction. The specification of the charge against you is: that on the Sabbath, while conducting the worship of God, in the Colored Mission Sabbath School of the First Reformed Presbyterian Church, in Mary street, near Sixth street, Philadelphia, you used uninspired hymns, contrary to the 8th section of the 24th chapter of our Testimony, which says that the Psalms, to the exclusion of all *imitations* and uninspired compositions, are to be used in social worship.

Witnesses, George H. Stuart, Jr., Francis McBride, Miss Annie Wells, Miss Adams, Miss Helen Blair, Mrs. Elizabeth McIlwain.

With all this you are charged; and an opportunity is now offered of presenting your defence, if any such you have to make.

EPHRAIM YOUNG.

Philadelphia, April 23d, 1868.

That this is a correct copy of a document presented to the General Synod of the Reformed Presbyterian Church, is certified by
JOHN N. McLEOD,
Stated Clerk.

[No. VI.]

PROTEST AND APPEAL.

We, the undersigned, elders of the First Reformed Presbyterian Church, Philadelphia, protest against all the proceedings of this Session, in regard to the election for Trustees, held on the 6th ult., by the congregation of this church—

For the following reasons, viz.:

1st. Because the Session have no jurisdiction in this case.

2d. Because, notwithstanding their want of jurisdiction, they have attempted, unlawfully, to strike from the list of electors one hundred and twenty-seven names, and this without citation and without trial.

3d. Because no person can be legally deprived of his or her rights by any court, whether civil or ecclesiastical, without due process of law.

4th. Because the attempt to deprive these persons of their rights, and, at the same time, withhold from the congregation their names and the reasons for such deprivation, is arbitrary and unpresbyterial.

5th. Because, if these persons had been properly notified, and an opportunity had been afforded them before this court, they might have been able to give satisfactory reasons why their names should not have been stricken from the list of electors.

6th. Because it is a matter of public notoriety, that some, and, probably, all of these persons, received from those who are now contesting the election, a printed ticket and circular, soliciting their votes, thus recognizing their *right* and *duty* to vote that printed ticket.

7th. Because, if the persons to whom these tickets and circulars were sent by these contestants, were not qualified to vote, they ought not to have been tempted by them to do what was improper and unlawful.

And now, for these reasons, we appeal from the decision of this Session to the Reformed Presbytery of Philadelphia, by some, called the First Reformed Presbytery of Philadelphia, to meet in semi-annual Session on the 1st Tuesday of May, 1868.

A. S. McMURRAY,
ROBERT GUY.

Philadelphia, February 15th, 1868.

And further, we subjoin the following document, containing additional and cumulative reasons for appealing, as appellants, in this case.

We, the undersigned, elders of the First Reformed Presbyterian Church, Philadelphia, protest against any official action already taken, or hereafter attempted by this Session, in regard to the election for Trustees lately held by the congregation of this church—

For the following reasons, viz.:

1st. Because the extract from the minutes of the congregational meeting of the 6th inst., submitted to session on the 23d inst., is incorrect; and, even if correct, it has not yet been adopted by the congregation.

2d. Because only two votes were challenged during the election; and, as those who challenged them failed to assign reasons therefor, and as no further opposition was made to their reception, and as the tellers agreed to receive them, their legality cannot now be questioned.

3d. Because the charter of the church gives no power to the Session, officially, to revise or set aside an election, duly held by the congregation.

4th. Because the Session should not attempt to revise the list of electors now, as to their qualifications for voting, by being in church communion, after the election has taken place.

5th. Because, according to the above-mentioned extract, the correctness of the list of pew-holders is to be ascertained by the late Board of Trustees; and, as these were all candidates for re-election, they should not revise the list after the ballot has been taken, inasmuch as this would constitute them judges of their own election.

6th. Because there is no authority anywhere now to strike from the list of electors any person not before dealt with and suspended from the privileges of the church, as evidenced by the minutes of this Session.

A. S. McMURRAY,
ROBERT. GUY.

Philadelphia, January 31st, 1868.

That this is a correct copy of a document presented to the General Synod of the Reformed Presbyterian Church, is certified by   JOHN N. McLEOD,

Stated Clerk.

[No. VII.]

PROTEST AND APPEAL.

REV. FATHERS AND BRETHREN :—We, the undersigned, elders of the First Reformed Presbyterian Church, Philadelphia, protest against the conduct of the First Reformed, by some, called the Reformed Presbytery of Philadelphia, on the 12th inst., in the matter of our joint Declinature, Protest and Appeal, then formally presented, and hereby signify our intention to appeal to General Synod, at the first meeting, of which intention public intimation was given at the time—

For the following reasons, viz.:

1st. Because, on presenting our Declinature, the Moderator, usurping the power of the court, proceeded to examine the docu ment himself, and afterwards made comments upon it before the Presbytery and a promiscuous assembly, which were partial, offensive, and insulting.

2d. Because, when our Protest against the action of Session was presented, the Moderator urged us to take back our Declinature, and we, refusing, he pronounced our refusal an insult to the court, and assigned this as a reason for not even opening our Protest and Appeal; and when, at this juncture, we protested, and appealed to General Synod, the Moderator declared from the Chair, that we "*had no* right to protest or appeal, *not being members of court,*" the rest acquiescing, in violation of our unquestionable rights. See Book of Discipline, section 3d, paragraph 5th.

3d. Because we, under a threat from the Chair of expulsion by the Sexton, were not permitted to utter one word in prosecution of our cause; and when the question was asked, had our Declinature been presented to Session within legal time, a member of court was permitted to give a lengthy answer in the negative, although intimation had been given by us *apud acta.*

4th. Because, in contravention of established ecclesiastical law, two individuals were recognized as members of court, against whom grave charges had been preferred by formal libel.

For these reasons, and others, contained in the accompanying documents, we appeal to your venerable body, and respectfully ask for such redress as you can give, according to the standards and established order of the church.

A. S. McMURRAY,
ROBERT GUY.

Philadelphia, May 20th, 1868.

That this is a correct copy of a document presented to the General Synod of the Reformed Presbyterian Church, is certified by JOHN N. McLEOD,

Stated Clerk.

[No. VIII.]

DECLINATURE.

The undersigned, elders of the First Reformed Presbyterian Church, Philadelphia, *decline* the pretended authority of the remanent members of session, in their unlawful attempt to exercise judicial powers, by affecting to pass censure upon them—

For the following reasons, viz. :

1st. Because three of the members of Session, viz.: George H. Stuart, James Grant, and Wm. John Chambers, have been subjected to grave charges, by formal libels preferred against them before Session, when in its full integrity, April 23d, 1868.

2d. Because, with the concurrence of two of the above-mentioned disqualified elders, the third being absent, they attempted, in violation of Presbyterial and social order, to pass censure upon one of us; and as a further outrage and open insult, they appointed the aforesaid three elders to prepare charges against the other.

3d. Because we cannot, in any degree, sanction the profanation of the name of the *Church's Head,* or the prostitution of any of the laws of his House, by such illegal and tyrannical proceedings.

And now, for these reasons, they appeal to the Reformed Presbytery of Philadelphia, by some, called the First Reformed Presbytery of Philadelphia, to meet in semi-annual Session on Tuesday, May 5th, 1868.

A. S. McMURRAY,
ROBERT GUY.

Philadelphia, May 4th, 1868.

That this is a correct copy of a document presented to the General Synod of the Reformed Presbyterian Church, is certified by   JOHN N. McLEOD,

Stated Clerk.

[No. IX.]

PROTEST AND APPEAL.

The undersigned, one of the members of the First Reformed Presbyterian Church, Philadelphia, protests against all the proceedings of this court in the cases of Geo. H. Stuart and James Grant, against whom I preferred charges on April 23d, 1868—

For the following reasons, viz. :

1st. Because all the courts of Christ's house, according to Presbyterial order, should be open to any of the members of the church who wish to attend, and none should sit with closed doors, unless under very peculiar circumstances; yet you rudely ordered myself, and three other brethren who accompanied me, to withdraw. With which order we complied, after your explicit promise to call in Geo. Gordon and myself before adjourning.

2d, Because, notwithstanding your promise, you were about to adjourn, although reminded of it by Mr. Henry Sterling, that venerable man who, a few hours afterwards, was so suddenly called to his eternal reward.

3d, Because, when we were invited in again by one of the members of court, who saw that the motion for adjournment was passed, even after Mr. Sterling's expostulation, you refused to receive my papers; and, after I had laid them on your table, and given notice of my Protest and appeal to the Philadelphia Reformed Presbytery, the Moderator contemptuously and violently threw them in my face.

4th, Because, at the previous regular meeting of Session, you adjourned, to meet at the call of the Moderator; and as no special business was mentioned by him in the announcement of the next meeting from the pulpit, the presentation of these papers was perfectly legitimate; and your solemn promise to admit us, and to attend to our business before the adjournment of the court, was an admission of this, and placed you under an additional obligation to receive them.

And now, for these reasons, I protest against the decision of this Session, in refusing to receive and act upon the above papers, and appeal to the Reformed Presbytery of Philadelphia, by some, called the First Reformed Presbytery of Philadelphia, to meet in semi-annual Session on the 1st Tuesday of May, 1868.

EPHRAIM YOUNG.

Philadelphia, May 1st, 1868.

That this is a correct copy of a document presented to the General Synod of the Reformed Presbyterian Church, is certified by 　　　　　　　　　　　　JOHN N. McLEOD,

Stated Clerk.

[No. X.]

PROTEST AND APPEAL.

The undersigned, one of the members of the First Reformed Presbyterian Church, Philadelphia, protests against all the proceedings of this Court, in the case of Wm. J. Chambers, against whom I preferred charges on April 23d, 1868. For the following reasons, viz.:

1st. Because all the Courts of Christ's house, according to Presbyterial order, should be open to any of the members of the church who wish to attend, and none should sit with closed doors unless under very peculiar circumstances; yet you rudely ordered myself and three other brethren who accompanied me to withdraw, with which order we complied after your explicit promise to call in Ephraim Young and myself before adjourning.

2d. Because, notwithstanding your promise, you were about to adjourn, although reminded of it by Mr. Henry Sterling, that venerable man who a few hours afterward was so suddenly called to his eternal reward.

3d. Because when we were invited in again by one of the members of the Court, who saw that the motion for adjournment was pressed, even after Mr. Sterling's expostulation, you refused to receive my paper; and after I had laid it on your table, and given notice of my protest and appeal to the Philadelphia Reformed Presbytery, the Moderator contemptuously and violently threw it, with others, in the face of Ephraim Young.

4th. Because at the previous regular meeting of Session you adjourned to meet at the call of the Moderator, and as no special business was mentioned by him in the announcement of the next meeting from the pulpit, the presentation of my paper was perfectly legitimate, and your solemn promise to admit us and attend to our business before the adjournment of the Court was an admission of this, and placed you under an additional obligation to receive it.

And now for these reasons I Protest against the decision of this Session, in refusing to receive and act upon the above paper, and appeal to the Reformed Presbytery of Philadelphia—by some called the First Reformed Presbytery of Philadelphia—to meet in semi-annual session on the first Tuesday of May, 1868.

GEORGE GORDON.

Philadelphia, May 1st, 1868.

That this is a correct copy of a document presented to the General Synod of the Reformed Presbyterian Church, is certified by

JOHN N. McLEOD, *Stated Clerk.*

PROTEST AND APPEAL.

Rev. Fathers and Brethren:

We the undersigned members of the First Ref. Pres. Church Phila., protest against the conduct of the First Ref. by some called the Reformed Presbytery of Philadelphia, on the 12th and 14th inst., in the matter of Protests against the illegal proceedings of the session of the First Ref. Pres. Church, Phila., in the case of certain libels, tabled before them on the 23d of April, 1868. For the following reasons, viz.:

1. Because apparently to screen the character of some, and injure the character of others, the Court went into secret session.

2. Because contrary to Rule 32d for the direction of judicatories in the Ref. Pres. Church our Protests were given into the hands of a committee.

3d. Because we were not allowed to offer any explanation or defense of our cause contrary to the inspired rule, which says "Doth our law judge any man before it hear him?"

4. Because two illegal members were permitted to judge in our case, and one of these was appointed on the committee to report on our papers thus vitiating the whole proceedings.

For these reasons and others in the accompanying documents we appeal to you, Fathers and Brethren, to render judgment in the premises, and rebuke such illegal proceedings.

GEORGE GORDON,
EPHRAIM YOUNG,

Philadelphia, May 20, 1868.

That this is a correct copy of a document presented to the General Synod of the Reformed Presbyterian Church, is certified by JOHN N. McLEOD,

Stated Clerk.

On the morning of May 23d, when these papers were referred to the Committee of Discipline, the following protest was entered:

[C]

PROTEST.

The subscribers respectfully protest against the action of the General Synod in receiving certain papers relating to the affairs of the First Reformed Presbyterian Church, Philadelphia, because,

1. Each and all of these papers came before Synod in a grossly irregular manner, and this not in any degree through the neglect or error of either the Reformed Presbytery of Philadelphia, or the Session of the First Reformed Presbyterian Church, Philadelphia. Paper No. 1, styled a Remonstrance, is (1) virtually and really a complaint against the pastor, the session, the trustees, and some of the most respected members of said First Reformed Presbyterian Church, Philadelphia, containing the most serious charges, which'were never presented to the persons accused, and which they never had any opportunity of preparing to meet. (2.) In every paragraph of said Remonstrance there are one or more shocking violations of truth. (3.) There is no evidence that the persons, whose names are appended to the paper, are in regular standing in connection with the congregation. (4.) It has been ascertained, by a slight examination, made by the Moderator and other members of the session now present at Synod, that several of the signers are persons under suspension, several under process, and some have withdrawn from the congregation, and a large number are not in regular standing. (5.) There is reason to believe that a considerable number of the persons who signed this Remonstrance never saw it or heard it.

Papers Nos. 3, 4 and 5 being sundry libels, were never received by the Session of the First Church, were not prepared or presented by that court, and were never heard by any member of it, until read in Synod.

Papers Nos. 6 and 7, protests of A. S. M'Murray and R. Guy, are irregular, because against action which session took in conjunction with Board of Trustees as arbitrators or referees, at the request of the congregation, and which cannot come under the supervision of this court, as the congregation never requested this court to consider the subject.

Paper No. 8, Declinature of R. Guy and A. S. M'Murray, was never presented to the Session, as required by the Book of Discipline. Ch. 3, § 3, p. 22, ed. 1865.

Papers No. 9, 10. Protest and Appeal of E. Young and G. Gordon were sent with proper replies to the Philadelphia Reformed Presbytery, which has them still under consideration.

2. These papers, containing the most serious charges against

persons of the most respectable character, were allowed to be read publicly in Synod, and no opportunity was given to reply to them, the previous question being put and carried.

3. Because there is evidence that these papers were prompted by malicious feelings, since there is reason to believe that not one of them would have been presented had not the session, after long patience, prepared to exercise discipline on several persons who were the disturbers of the peace of the congregation.

4. Because to receive such papers tends to destroy and not to support the just authority of the Presbytery, and the Session to whose jurisdiction the persons purporting to present these papers are subject.

Samuel Wylie,		T. W. J. Wylie,
John F. Hill,	So far as it	A. G. McAuley,
Robt. McMillan,	relates to the	R. H. MacMunn,
Benj. Miller,	irregularity of	W. Sterrett,
Geo. Scott,	the papers.	Geo. H. Stuart.
John McMillan,		

CASE OF MR. GEO. H. STUART.

On Monday, May 25th, James Sample, Ruling Elder of Brooklyn, N. Y., presented the following Resolutions:

WHEREAS, Geo. H. Stuart has for a long time been pursuing divisive courses and whereas he did, on the 22d inst., openly and defiantly avow on the floor of General Synod that he had violated the standards of the church on Psalmody and Communion and would continue to do so, therefore

Resolved, That Geo. H. Stuart be and he hereby is suspended from the Eldership and Membership of the Reformed Presbyterian church, and his seat in the Synod consequently vacated.

JAMES SAMPLE.

On Tuesday, May 26th, S. B. W. McLeod, M. D., Ruling Elder New York City, offered the following amendment to the pending Resolution:

WHEREAS, Mr. Geo. H. Stuart, a member of this Synod, has given that honor and place to human compositions which are due only to the Book of Psalms; has engaged in communion with persons, and in a manner condemned by the church to which he belongs; has very extensively withdrawn his support from this church, has on two occasions in open Synod defied the authority of Synod, and challenged official notice thereof; has often thrown or attempted to throw odium and ridicule on our denomination; has distinctly int he opinions of intelligent persons outside as well as among ourselves, followed divisive courses, and used his means and influences so to do, and has in the prosecution of his apparent purpose in breaking down the church, extensively sown discord among brethren, therefore

Resolved, That a commitee of Synod be appointed to confer with Mr. Stuart, and should he pledge himself to the satisfaction of Synod to alter his conduct in these respects, that the disapproval by Synod of his past actions be expressed by the Moderator, and the matter be dismissed. But should he not consent to this, that he be suspended from the exercise of his office and membership until restored by Synod or a commission thereof.

On the afternoon of May 26th, Mr. Robert Matthews offered the following substitute for the pending resolution and amendment:

WHEREAS, Mr. Geo. H. Stuart, upon his own acknowledgment, on the floor of this Synod, has used in the worship of God other songs, as the matter of praise, than those authorized by this Synod; and,

WHEREAS, He has departed from the order of the church in the matter of communion; therefore,

Resolved 1. That Mr. Stuart be required to promise conformity hereafter to the usages of our historically venerable church, on these points; and that he receive an admonition from the Moderator.

Resolved 2. That in case Mr. Stuart will not submit to this mild censure, he be suspended from his privileges in the church, and his seat declared vacant in this Synod.

The Moderator put the question, Shall the substitute be enter tained ? It was decided in the negative.

On May 27th, Rev. A. G. Wylie offered a substitute for all the papers before the house in Mr. Stuart's case. It was entertained.

WHEREAS, This Synod possesses original as well as appellate jurisdiction over all persons and all matters affecting the general interests of the church, under its supervision and care; and

WHEREAS, There are well-known and established laws in regard to the subjects of Psalmody and Communion, in the former of which an inspired Psalmody, to the exclusion of all imitations and uninspired compositions, is to be used in the worship of God; and in the latter, declaring Communion in sealing ordinances to be extended to those only whom we would receive to constant fellowship, and become subject to the authority of this Church; and

WHEREAS, George H. Stuart has openly and defiantly declared on various occasions, and on the floor of this Synod, that he has, in the worship of God, used imitations and uninspired compositions, called hymns; and that he has communed with others, and in other churches, in sealing ordinances, and has declared that he will continue so to do; therefore

Resolved, 1st. That by this avowed course of conduct, George H. Stuart has violated the laws of this church, in these cases made and provided.

Resolved, 2d. That George H. Stuart be and hereby is suspended from his office, and from membership in this church, until he acknowledge his error in the premises, and submit to the laws and authority of this church, and that his seat in Synod, in consequence, be declared vacated.

A. G. WYLIE.

I hereby certify that the above is a correct copy of the substitute offered for all relating to the matter before Synod in the case of George H. Stuart.

NEVIN WOODSIDE,
Assistant Clerk.

Dr. Wylie presented the following paper, which was read, and ordered on record:

To the Moderator of the General Synod of the Reformed Presbyterian Church in session at Pittsburgh, May, 1868.

I hereby solemnly deny each and all of the allegations and charges contained in the preamble and resolutions offered by Rev. A. G. Wylie, in manner and form as they are alleged, and I protest against the right of Synod to pass such preamble and resolutions, and ask that this my denial and protest be entered on the minutes.

GEO. H. STUART.

Pittsburgh, May 28, 1868.

Synod proceeded to vote. The roll was called and result declared as follows: Ayes—The Moderator, W. S. Bratton, Dr.

Crawford, Dr. Douglas, M. Harshaw, J. F. Morton, W. J. McDowell, Dr. McMaster, A. Thomson, N. Woodside, A. G. Wylie, S. Young, W. Earley, J. N. Gifford, Peter Gibson, K. Hunter, R. Hemphill, J. Holmes, R. Matthews, R. Marshall, W. McLachlan, W. Reed, D. Fields, D. Stewart, J. Sample, J. Stormont, M. Shirra, J. Scott—28.*

Noes—J. H. Cooper, J. F. Hill, Thomas Johnston, Dr. McLeod, J. McMillan, R. McMillan, Dr. McAuley, Dr. Scott, Dr. Sterrett, S. Wylie, Dr. Wylie, H. Dehaven, B. Miller, R. H. MacMunn—14.

Not voting—Dr. Clarke, A. R. Gailey, W. P. Shaw, A. Kerr, W. McCormick, J. Stewart—6.

The Moderator announced that the preamble and resolutions were adopted; and declared that Mr. G. H. Stuart was suspended from office and membership in the Reformed Presbyterian Church.

[D]

PROTEST AGAINST ACTION OF GENERAL SYNOD IN CASE OF GEO. H. STUART.

1. Because assuming that the Synod possesses the original jurisdiction it claims, this jurisdiction can be exercised only on the conditions and according to the order established in its own Book of Discipline, which it has violated in every particular. Ch. 3rd. § 2, pp. 3, 5, 6, 7, 8, 9, 10, 11.

2. Because the form of the charges against Mr. Stuart was changed three several times, said charges being first presented in a resolution by James Sample; then in an amendment to said resolution by Dr.S. B. W. McLeod; then, finally, in a substitute for the whole subject presented by Rev. A. G. Wylie.

3. Because at the time of the introduction of said resolution by Rev A. G. Wylie, Mr. Stuart was confined to his room in the Monongahela House in the city of Pittsburg, with a violent attack of spasmodic Asthma, which rendered it impossible for him to attend Synod, without danger of his life, as he was advised by his physi-

---

*Dr. McLeod, who as Clerk of Synod, called the roll, arranged in alphabetical order, omitted his own name in its regular place, and although attention was called to this by several members, he refused to declare his vote until all the other members of Synod had voted.

cian, James King, M. D., whose certificate to this effect was publicly read before the Synod.*

4. Because Mr. G. H. Stuart was never notified of the resolution under which he was suspended.

5. Because the only official notice received by Mr. Stuart was the following namely: "The following resolution was passed by the General Synod of the Ref. Pres. Church, at its session in Pittsburg, May 27, 1868. Attest John N. McLeod, Stated Clerk. Resolved, That the vote on the pending question (in the case of Mr. Geo. H. Stuart) be taken at ¼ to 12 o'clock M. this day, and that Mr. Stuart be informed of this by the Stated Clerk. Pittsburg, May 27th, 1868," which notice was not served on Mr. Stuart until about ¼ before 11 A. M., on Thursday, May 28th.

6. Because after service of the aforesaid notice but before the vote on said preamble and resolution, namely, at or about ¼ past 12 o'clock P. M., May 28th, Mr. G. H. Stuart, through Dr. T. W. J. Wylie presented to the Moderator of the Synod a paper solemnly denying each and all of the allegations and charges contained in said preamble and resolutions in manner and form as alleged, and protesting against the right of Synod to pass the same, and yet notwithstanding said denial and protest without giving Mr. Stuart any opportunity of being heard in his defense the Synod proceeded to take a vote on said Preamble and Resolutions and passed them.

7. Because the particular acts charged against Mr. Geo. H. Stuart have been allowed for many years in the Ref. Pres. Church, while well known to Synod.

8. Because several other members of Synod publicly declared on the floor of Synod that they had done the things with which Mr. Stuart was charged, and no censure was proposed or passed on them.

9. Because there is no evidence that Mr. Stuart's practice as

---

*CERTIFICATE FROM DR. KING.

PITTSBURGH, *May 27th*, 1868.

I certify that Mr. Geo. H. Stuart is now under my professional care for a violent attack of spasmodic asthma. I have advised him to remain in his room until he can leave the city, wh ch I think he should do as soon as possible. I do not hesitate to say that he cannot attend the session of Synod, with which he is connected, this afternoon, without danger to his life, and I have advised him accordingly.

Very respectfully,

JAMES KING, M.D.

admitted by him, although not in the form and manner alleged, is contrary to a proper interpretation of the standards of the Ref. Pres. Church.

10. Because the terms of ecclesiastical communion in the Reformed Presbyterian Church require assent to our standards only "as embodying, according to the Word of GOD, *the great principles* of the Covenanted Presbyterian Reformation."

11. Because the formula of queries to be put to Ministers and Ruling Elders at ordination requires assent to the standards of the Reformed Presbyterian Church only, "as embodying the great principles of the Covenanted Reformation."

12. Because the passage of said resolution is calculated to produce great detriment to the Reformed Presbyterian Church.

13. Because the passage of the Resolution will produce great detriment to religion.

14. Because Mr. G. H. Stuart's eminent labors and services in the cause of the Lord Jesus Christ, for the Church at large and this Church in particular, for the welfare of all classes and conditions of men, for the cause of missions at home and abroad, and especially on behalf of our soldiers during the recent struggle, greatly aggravated the injustice and wickedness with which he has been treated.

SAMUEL WYLIE,	A. G. MCAULEY,
T. W. J. WYLIE,	ROBT. MCMILLAN,
W. STERRETT,	JOHN F. HILL,
GEO. SCOTT.	R. H.MACMUNN,
	BENJ. MILLER,
	JOHN MCMILLAN.

On the 29th of May, the Report of the Committee of Discipline was adopted, as follows:

REPORT OF THE COMMITTEE OF DISCIPLINE.

The Committee on Discipline respectfully report to General Synod in relation to the papers presented by Elders, Trustees and Members of the First Reformed Presbyterian Congregation of Philadelphia, as follows:

The remonstrance, which is also a petition for a redress of

grievances, being addressed to Synod, comes up regularly for consideration. The other papers, although not coming technically, according to the rules, should not, on this account, be pronounced irregular, inasmuch as any seeming irregularity which attaches to them does not arise from any disregard of the rules of order on the part of those by whom they are presented, but the failure on the part of Session of the First Reformed Presbyterian Church, Philadelphia, and the Reformed Presbytery of Philadelphia, to take action upon them.

In view of all the circumstances of the case, the Committee recommend the adoption of the following resolutions:

Resolved, 1st. That the act of suspension pronounced by the Session of the First Reformed Presbyterian Congregation of Philadelphia, on Dr. A. S. McMurray and Mr. Robert Guy, and the same is hereby revoked.

Resolved, 2d. That the joint action of the Session and Board of Trustees of the First Reformed Presbyterian Congregation of Philadelphia, in disfranchising or declaring illegal the votes of one hundred and twenty-seven members or adherents thereto, who voted at the last annual election for Trustees in said congregation, without issuing a citation upon them, or allowing them a hearing, is contrary to the good order of the laws of God's house, be and the same is hereby declared illegal and of no effect.

Resolved, 3d. That the whole matter pertaining to the difficulties existing in the First Reformed Presbyterian Church of Philadelphia, be referred to a Commission of General Synod, to be appointed by the Moderator, consisting of four ministers and three ruling elders, who shall be clothed with Synodical powers and have authority to issue the whole case.

Resolved, 4th. That this Commission, of whom any three ministers and any two ruling elders shall constitute a quorum, shall meet in the First Reformed Presbyterian Church, Philadelphia, on ———* day of June, 1868, at 3 o'clock, P. M., and shall continue their Sessions from day to day, or by adjournment from time to time, until they shall have investigated and issued the whole case.

Resolved, 5th. That the Session of the First Reformed Presby-

---

* The blank was afterwards filled by the appointment of June 17th, 1868, at 3.30, P.M.

terian Congregation of Philadelphia, consisting of Rev. Dr. T. W. J. Wylie, Moderator, and Messrs. G. H. Stuart, A. S. McMurray, Robert Guy, James Grant, J. P. Smith, W. J. Chambers, William Ray, members, be, and are hereby suspended and restrained from the exercise of judicial functions in any matter or matters pertaining to the present difficulties in said congregation, or considering and issuing, in their judicial capacity as a Session, any case relating to said difficulties.

Resolved, 6th. That the Philadelphia Reformed Presbytery be, and hereby are restrained and prohibited from considering or issuing any case now pending before them, or that may hereafter be brought before them, relating to the existing difficulties in the First Reformed Presbyterian Congregation of Philadelphia.

Resolved, 7th. That the decision of the Commission, subject to the review of General Synod at its next regular meeting, shall be final ; and none of the parties shall plead or be impleaded either in Session or Presbytery, on any of the matters connected with of arising out of the present existing difficulties, until such review shall have been made, and the disabilities imposed above, in regard to the exercise of judicial functions, shall have been removed.

Resolved, 8th. That all the papers presented to General Synod on the subject, be referred to the Synodical Commission, to be appointed as above.

Pittsburg, May 27th, 1868.

I hereby certify that the above is a true copy.

JOHN N. McLEOD, *Stated Clerk*
General Synod of the Reformed Presbyterian Church.

At the afternoon session, May 29th, Rev. Dr. M'Master, Rev. Dr. Douglas, Rev. A. G. Wylie, Rev. W. J. McDowell, and Ruling Elders, James Stewart, Thomas Smith, William McLachlan, were appointed the Commission of Synod.

[E]
PROTEST AGAINST ADOPTION OF REPORT OF COM. MITTEE ON DISCIPLINE.

The subscribers respectfully protest against adoption of Report of Committee on Discipline, Because 1. There is no provision for referring such matters to a commission clothed with such powers.

2. Because several of the matters referred to are already in the hands of a Commission appointed by the Reformed Presbytery of Philadelphia, and have not in any regular way been removed from said commission to the Synod.

3. Because not one of the papers in which these subjects were presented came before Synod in a regular form.

4. Because the 1st Resolution performs a judicial act without pursuing any judicial forms.

5. Because the 2d Resolution undertakes to deal with a subject over which the Synod has no jurisdiction.

6. Because the 5th and 6th disregard the conditions and forms required in the removal of cases to the jurisdiction of the General Synod, which properly belong to the inferior judicatories.

SAMUEL WYLIE,
T. W. J. WYLIE,
B. MILLER,
JOHN F. HILL.

A. G. MCAULEY,
W. STERRETT,
R. H. MACMUNN,
GEO. SCOTT,
JOHN MCMILLAN,
R. MCMILLAN.

APPENDIX.

[Several documents connected with the preceding, which would have been presented to Synod or Presbytery, had the case come up in a regular manner, are published in this Appendix.]

[No. I.]

ADDRESS BY THE PASTOR OF THE FIRST RE-FORMED PRESBYTERIAN CHURCH.

(READ FROM THE PULPIT, MAY 3, 1868.)

Dear Brethren and Friends:—You are aware that the peace of our congregation has been, for some time past, sadly disturbed. Remarkable, until recently, for the love and good feeling which prevailed amongst us, the question arises, what has caused so great, so melancholy a change? We believe it may be traced to the circulation of the most unwarrantable representations, that some change in our mode of worship was contemplated, and that the Psalmody which we now employ, venerable for its age, endeared by many hallowed associations, and which has been to such multitudes the expression of their holiest and most delightful emotions, was to be thrust aside. We do not wonder that this should prove so exciting, but let us *again* assure you, as we have done before, that nothing could be more untrue. So far as we are aware, there is not one member of the Session, or of the Board of Trustees, or of the entire congregation, who has had any design or expectation of this kind. Disregard, we pray you, as a gross calumny, any such representation.

It is now about a year since such rumors began to circulate, having at that time reference to some conjectured action of our General Synod. The representation then made that something of this sort was contemplated, we believe was a mere fabrication, as nothing whatever of that sort was proposed. Yet many were thus deceived, and signed a memorial which we believe was really designed to rally a party, and form a base for future movements. When the year was about to close, and the election for Trustees was approaching, it was ascertained that some change in the Board would be attempted, by which long-tried and eminently trustworthy members were to be superseded. Numbers were told that if certain persons, who had served the congregation for many years, should be reëlected, "the Psalms would be put out," and that, if they wished to retain the Psalms, they should vote for other persons. As not one of the persons objected to was in favor of changing our Psalmody, and as the Board of Trustees had not the power to do it, even if they desired, there could scarcely be a greater untruth, and yet in this way many were deceived. When the election took place, amidst scenes of disorder never before witnessed, and which we trust will never occur again, it was observed that many persons voted whose right to do so was questionable. The legality of such votes was very properly referred to the Session and Board of Trustees, who alone were competent to decide in the matter. Meanwhile it was the *duty* of the former Board of Trustees to retain the control of the church property. They were bound to deliver it to their lawfully elected successors, and till it was decided who were their lawfully elected successors they were bound to retain its custody. Such has been the decision of the Chief Justice, and such would be the decision in any court of law whatever. Let it be observed that it is not a *Minority* Board holding the church as against a *Majority* Board, but the Board which now holds the church, is a Board whose election has not been questioned, and a majority of the members of which form also a majority of the members of the Board claiming office for the present year. And yet, while the matter was undetermined, before any decision had been given, or could have been given by the Session and Board of Trustees, to whom the subject was referred, the Board of Trustees claiming to be elected, hastily and rashly rushed into a *law suit*, against their brethren, disregarding even the fact that they had thus referred the matter to the civil law. Without waiting for its decision, they attempted to collect pew-rents, and it was necessary to restrain them by an injunction. And now, as the Supreme Court in Banc, by which alone a final decision can be given, will not meet in this district till January next, the suit cannot be decided until after another election shall have taken place, and thus, even if it were decided in their favor, they could gain nothing, as their term of office will have ended.

And now, dear brethren, we beg you to consider whether the continuation of this controversy can have any other effect than to distract, divide, and perhaps destroy our congregation. It is not needed in order to maintain our present *Psalmody*—no one thinks of changing it. It has no bearing on the subject of *Union* with other churches, for that union may not take place for many years, and could not take place at any time without regular ecclesiastical action.

The Session has waited and pleaded with the leaders in this matter, but all attempts at conciliation have failed. A compromise has been proposed by filling as they would desire the vacancy in the old Board of Trustees, arising from the death of our dear friend and brother, Mr. D. W. Denison. It is refused. They have been urged to abandon a fruitless lawsuit, which can result only in squandering the money of those who think proper to contribute to it. Yet this lawsuit is persisted in. The offer has been made of an amicable division of the congregation, and a generous proportion of the value of the church property, although it is well known that the amount contributed for it, by those who are concerned in this movement is but small compared with that which those who sustain the old Board had given. But all has been of no avail. We must still be agitated and distracted; our peace disturbed; our spiritual improvement and enjoyment prevented.— And for what purpose? We can see nothing else than to drive off from the church those who have been both in earlier and later years its best supporters, its most worthy members; and *with them myself.* Do not misunderstand us, dear brethren; we do not mean that the great mass of the adherents of this movement entertain any such design, but they are led, by false representations, to take sides with those whose conduct can produce no other result than this. Outside influences have been at work. We have become obnoxious to some of our brethren because we conscientiously opposed them. We must be crushed, and discord is sown; dissension fomented; strife promoted; our congregation is to be divided; ourselves to be driven out. Let those who condemn such conduct separate themselves from those whose course can have no other effect.

With these things, dear brethren, we have borne in the hope that forbearance would induce a change, but we have been disappointed. The congregation is distracted, our prayer-meetings are disturbed, the services of the Sabbath interrupted, our communion cannot be held, the private meetings of the session are invaded. What could we do? We have borne too long. That venerable man whose sudden death we all so much regret, one so amiable, so kind, so meek, so upright, so intelligent, so judicious, so conscientious, so eminently *good*, has repeatedly urged the Session to exercise the discipline of the church in regard to the men who trouble us. We have at length felt obliged to do so, and four persons have been put under process, of whom one, Dr. A. S. McMurray, has been suspended according to the direction of our Book of Discipline "till his trial comes on and while it is pending." It is not our intention to proceed hastily, but to all who may appear before us, we design to give a full, fair, and open trial, and were these persons now or at any time to indicate a disposition to cease from agitation or disturbing our peace, how gladly would we welcome this, and how heartily receive them again!

And now, dear brethren, we appeal to you to sustain the constituted authorities of the congregation. We have not been impatient—we have not been rash—we have not been malevolent. Regretting most deeply the necessity which required it, we have adopted this course to suppress discord and to promote peace. If you love your pastor, if you have any respect for the office-bearers of the church, whether living or departed—if you desire peace—if you wish to promote the interests of religion and the glory of GOD our Saviour—we beseech you to give no countenance or encouragement to any designing or disorderly men who may endeavor to keep up strife and discord among us. If they ask you to sign any paper under whatever pretext decline to do so. Deceived as many have been already, let none be deceived again.

And now, brethren, for the first time in our pastorate, permit us to address to you a personal appeal. No one surely can feel a deeper interest in your welfare than we do. Our loved and honored father was your first pastor, and continued so for nearly fifty years. We have felt as if he had left to us in you a most precious trust, which we should deliver unimpaired to the one who may succeed us. How can we bear to think of the flock, "the beautiful flock," for which he labored and prayed so earnestly, so faithfully, so long, becoming divided and destroyed? Ourselves, your own child and offspring, born among you, with you in the sanctuary from infancy, a pupil in your Sabbath-school the first day it was organized, afterwards a teacher there—permitted more than thirty years ago to sit down with you at the Saviour's table to commemorate His dying love, called by your unanimous voice to be your pastor nearly twenty-five years ago, about half our life-time—ever heard by you with respect, and received in your houses with affection—ever sustained by you with most generous kindness—ever receiving the greatest forbearance for our many, many deficiencies and faults— we have felt that you were "our joy and our crown." And shall unfounded suspicions, shall any misconception of motives and purposes destroy our confidence and love?—alienate and separate those who might still be as harmonious and as peaceful and as happy as they have been before! May God forbid! These six things the Lord hateth, yea, seven are an abomination unto Him— "a proud look, a lying tongue, hands that shed innocent blood, an heart that deviseth wicked imaginations, feet that be swift in running to mischief, a false witness that speaketh lies, and he *that soweth discord among brethren.*" "Mark those who cause divisions and avoid them." "Follow peace with all men and holiness, without which no man shall see the Lord." "Let us follow after the things which make for peace and things wherewith one may edify another." "And now may the God of Peace which brought again from the dead our Lord Jesus, that great Shepherd of the sheep, through the blood of the everlasting covenant, make you perfect in every good work, to do his will, working in you that which is well pleasing in his sight, through Jesus Christ, to whom be glory for ever and ever. Amen."

[No. II.]

STATEMENT IN REGARD TO PROTEST AND APPEAL OF McMURRAY AND GUY.

(To be Presented to the Reformed Presbytery of Philadelphia, if called for.)

The Session of the First Reformed Presbyterian Church of Philadelphia very respectfully submit to the Reformed Presbytery of Philadelphia the following statement in regard to a Protest and Appeal of Dr. A. S. McMurray and Mr. R. Guy, which we have informed these brethren we have declined to send up to your venerable body.

1. We desire that it be distinctly understood that it is by no means with the intention of depriving these brethren of the opportunity of being heard on the subject before your venerable court, as we have informed them, that they may accomplish this by a *complaint* against us in these premises.

2. The subject to which the Protest and Appeal relates came before us by a vote of the congregation referring it to us, and we have considered that it could not come before Presbytery or Synod without a similar vote referring it to either of these bodies. We have no right to send it to Presbytery or Synod unless the congregation so desire and direct.

3. The subject to which it refers is not properly a spiritual matter. It is a civil transaction, being the right of voting under a charter from the government of the State, and this it is not for any ecclesiastical court to decide unless it be voluntarily submitted thereto by the party concerned.

4. As neither Presbytery nor Synod could assume cognizance of this matter without the congregation having referred it to either, so no action of either could receive the least attention in the legal settlement of the case.

5. As we do not consider that the Session had any right to act on this matter unless it had been referred to them, so we cannot refer the subject to the Presbytery or the Synod, as the congregation has not directed this to be done.

The Session begs leave to submit to Presbytery some remarks on the Protest and Appeal, of which a copy is appended.

I. As regards the first reason, viz.: "That this Session has no jurisdiction in this case." We admit that we had no ecclesiastical jurisdiction, and we affirm that we did not assume or exercise any. For

1. We acted in this matter only because it was respectfully referred to us by the congregation, and that it was thus referred we are prepared to prove,

(1.) By the official minutes of the meeting as certified to us by the Secretary thereof.

(2.) By the testimony of a great number of witnesses.

(3.) By the fact that the congregation adjourned twice to receive our report.

Unless the congregation had referred it to us we could not and would not have acted upon it.

2. We acted in this matter in conjunction with the Board of Trustees, who have no ecclesiastical power, and who could not and did not unite with us in any ecclesiastical act.

3. Over a large number of persons on the list of voters referred to us we had no jurisdiction whatever, as they were not members of the Church, and we certainly were not so ignorant as to claim or exercise any such jurisdiction.

4. We acted in this matter, therefore, simply as *arbitrators* or *referees*, and we maintain that not only had the congregation a right to refer it to us in conjunction with the Board of Trustees, in this character, but that it was eminently proper to do so, because

(1.) The congregation might have referred it to any other persons of intelligence and probity.

(2.) No others could so well ascertain the facts required in the case, as the Session and Trustees alone possessed the necessary documents.

(3.) Our Minutes will show that subjects of dispute among members of the congregation have frequently been brought before us by the parties concerned, in order to avoid litigation in the civil courts, but in no such case has it ever been supposed that our action was a proper subject for protest or appeal to a higher court.

II. The second reason, "Because we attempted unlawfully to strike from the list," &c. We reply that the election had been already held when our action on the subject was invoked, and we merely expressed the opinion, in conjunction with the Board of Trustees, that such persons, to the number of 127, had voted without being entitled to do so. We did not prevent any of these persons from voting, or strike their names from the list of electors. No list of electors had been made, and had it been made it would have legally included many more than those who actually voted. And in regard to "citation and trial," we observe that no citation or trial was necessary or proper, for

(1.) The duty of the Session in conjunction with the Board was simply to ascertain, for the benefit of the congregation and in reply to its application, what persons had a right to vote.

(2.) It was supposed that all or nearly all of those who had voted without the right to do so, had done this from a mistake, and no charges had been preferred before the Session against them.

(3.) Many of these persons were not members of the church and not under our jurisdiction, nor subject to citation from us or trial before us.

III. The third reason, "Because no person can be deprived," &c. We again observe that as the election had already taken place, we did not *deprive* any person of the right of voting, but merely in conjunction with the Trustees declared our opinion that such persons as we enumerated had voted *without* a right. As the act was already performed no process of law could prevent the performance of it, and we cannot see how any process of law could affect it. We gave our opinion with impartiality, integrity, great care and in the fear of GOD.

IV. The fourth reason, "Withholding names," &c. We observe,

1. The Session expressly stated that they were ready to satisfy any legitimate inquiry, and all persons seeking information have been or would be informed.

2. As it was believed that most of those on the list of persons not entitled to vote had voted without any idea that they had not a right, it was considered improper to expose them to public remark and perhaps misrepresentation, by announcing their names at the congregational meeting.

V. The fifth reason, " These persons might have been able to give," &c.

(1.) Nothing which any of these persons might do after the election could possibly constitute them electors if they were not so at or before that time.

(2.) The Session in conjunction with the Board of Trustees alone possessed the information necessary to decide the matter.

(3.) Many of these persons were not amenable to the Session and of some who voted, being neither members nor pew-holders, both the Session and Trustees have been and continue to be utterly ignorant.

VI. and VII. The sixth reason, " Because it is," &c. The seventh reason, " Because," &c. We observe,

1. That the Board of Trustees now holding possession of the church property and which is recognized by the pastor and Session, has not been contesting the election, but certain other persons claiming to have been elected, but whose election was submitted to the Session and Trustees by the congregation. Nor is the Board which holds possession of the church to be considered as a minority Board holding it against a majority Board, but it is the old Board whose election has never been disputed, and of which a majority of the members form also a majority of the Board claiming to have been elected; and it further would certainly have been wrong for the Board holding the church to surrender the possession of it to any other than its legitimately elected successors, and till it should be ascertained who were its legitimate successors it was the duty of the former Board to retain the property. It is also to be understood that those who are represented as the contestants in this Protest and Appeal are not the persons who have initiated and continued a vexatious law-suit, but that the persons who are really the contestants and have commenced this suit are the persons whose claim to be Trustees is maintained by these appellants.

2. With the conduct of those who prepared and distributed the printed ticket and circular this Session has nothing to do, but no act of these persons could be supposed to *determine* or even to *recognize* the right and duty of these to whom the circular was sent to vote, for the persons who sent the circular might send to any they pleased, and probably sent it to persons whom they knew not

to be voters. If sending a ticket and circular to any persons gives them a right to vote, it would be a very easy thing to manufacture voters.

3. The Session had no concern in this matter. Several of the members of session never saw either circular or ticket until they received it by the post, and the only member of Session who signed the circular was our venerable and beloved Father, Mr. Henry Sterling, who has so recently entered into his heavenly rest, and whose previous character for integrity, intelligence, mildness, and moderation might have shielded him from the reproach of having "tempted others to do what was improper and unlawful."

Signed by authority of the Session.

T. W. J. WYLIE, Moderator.

JAMES GRANT, Ass't. Clerk.

[No. III.]

COMPARATIVE STATEMENT OF CONTRIBUTIONS TO BUILDING FUND, ETC.

The entire cost of the Church building and ground on Broad Street was $65,720.23

Contributed as follows:

From proceeds sale of old church,	$12,883.25	
Subscriptions by members of congregation,	39,951.33	
Collected from friends by members,	12,885.65	
		65,720.23
Of the above amount the signers of the Remonstrance contributed	4,583.86	
Collected by them from their friends,	103.00	
		4,686.86

Showing that the signers of the Remonstrance contributed only 7⅓ per cent. of the total cost, or 8⅞ per cent. of the actual amount subscribed and collected towards the erection of the new church.

The total amount of Pew Rent collected for 1867 was $5,214.02

The amount of Pew Rent paid by the signers of the Remonstrance for 1867 was   1,319.92

Showing that the signers of the Remonstrance paid only 25¼ per cent. of the whole amount received.

The amount contributed by the congregation for Missionary purposes during the Synodical Year 1867–68 was $1,279.84

Of this sum the signers to the Remonstrance have contributed, so far as ascertained, by direct subscriptions $42.50

Estimating as the same in amount their contributions in Sabbath School and Monthly Concert collections   42.50

           ——— 85.00

It thus appears that their contributions in all are 6⅔ per cent. of the whole amount contributed for Missionary purposes by the congregation during the year ending May, 1868.

The number of persons in full communion and regular standing in the First Reformed Presbyterian Church, Philadelphia, January 1, 1868, was eight hundred and twenty-five. The number of signatures to the Remonstrance, deducting those improperly attached to it, is two hundred and eleven, or 25½ per cent. of the entire membership. It is worthy of remark that not one person connected with the original congregation, now surviving, and not a single representative of any family belonging to it, has signed the remonstrance.

www.ingramcontent.com/pod-product-compliance
Lightning Source LLC
Chambersburg PA
CBHW031819090426

42739CB00008B/1337